MAS P SELLER

THOMAS T. PEPPER   BOOKSELLER.

TOPPER

Pencils

THE TOPPER BOOK

Printed and Published by D. C. THOMSON & CO., LTD., 185 Fleet Street, London EC4A 2HS.

TRICKY DICKY

HA! YOU DON'T FOOL ME, DICKY!

SPLATT!

BAH! EVERYONE EXPECTS WINTER TRICKS FROM ME AT THIS TIME OF YEAR!

BUT—HEY!—THEY WOULDN'T EXPECT SUMMER TRICKS, WOULD THEY?

SOON—

EH? A DECK-CHAIR?

I'D BETTER PUT IT AWAY! NOBODY SITS OUT IN THIS WEATHER.

CLICK!

YAARGLE!

SNAP!

TWOING!

STUCK

GEMME OUTTA THIS!

HAW! HAW! MY SPRING-LOADED DECK-CHAIR CAUGHT YOU OUT!

ERK! WHAT'S THIS? A BUTTERFLY IN WINTER?

FLAP!

BZZT!

WRONG! IT'S A RADIO-CONTROLLED MOTH, ACTUALLY! HEE! HEE!

YIKES! MY TIE!

GNASH! GNASH!

PRESS!

THE *TREE SPOTTERS' GUIDE* NO 1

LEAF SPRAY with CONE.

NORWAY SPRUCE

FLOWERS

The SPRUCE FIR is an evergreen, cone-bearing tree, sometimes growing up to thirty metres high. The wood of this tree is often used to make flag-poles and pleasure-boat masts.

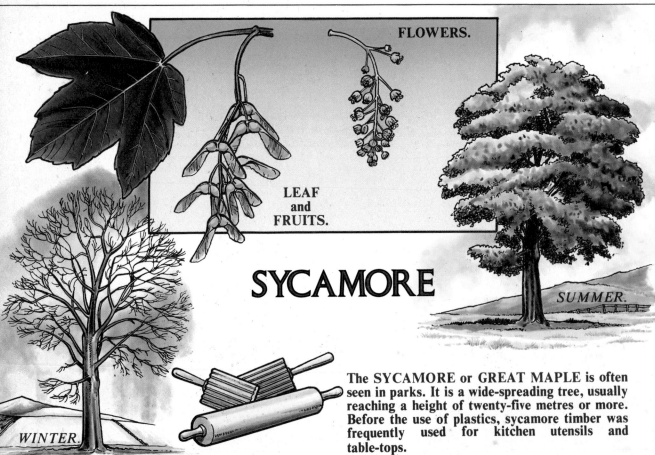

FLOWERS.

LEAF and FRUITS.

SYCAMORE

SUMMER.

WINTER.

The SYCAMORE or GREAT MAPLE is often seen in parks. It is a wide-spreading tree, usually reaching a height of twenty-five metres or more. Before the use of plastics, sycamore timber was frequently used for kitchen utensils and table-tops.

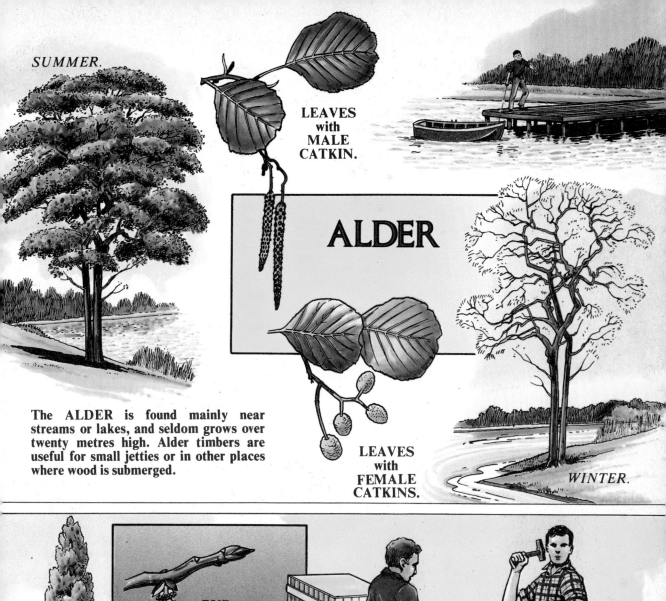

SUMMER.

LEAVES
with
MALE
CATKIN.

ALDER

LEAVES
with
FEMALE
CATKINS.

WINTER.

The ALDER is found mainly near streams or lakes, and seldom grows over twenty metres high. Alder timbers are useful for small jetties or in other places where wood is submerged.

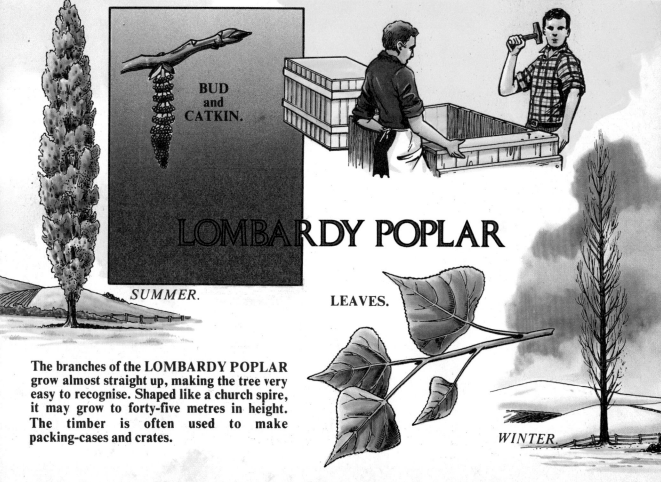

BUD
and
CATKIN.

LOMBARDY POPLAR

SUMMER.

LEAVES.

WINTER.

The branches of the LOMBARDY POPLAR grow almost straight up, making the tree very easy to recognise. Shaped like a church spire, it may grow to forty-five metres in height. The timber is often used to make packing-cases and crates.

Danny's Tranny

DANNY WILSON'S super tranny can make objects larger, smaller, lighter than air or invisible—but only for a short time.

COME ON, DANNY WILSON. LET ME HAVE A LOOK AT YOUR HOMEWORK ANSWERS.

OI! STOPPIT!

HURRY, DANNY. WE'LL BE LATE.

IT'S ALL BULLY BENSON'S FAULT. AND NOW HE'S GOT MY ANSWERS.

SOON...

SHRINKING RAY

WE'RE LATE, ALL RIGHT. BUT WITH MY TRANNY'S HELP, WE CAN SNEAK INTO CLASS.

OPEN YOUR HOMEWORK BOOKS, BOYS. I SHALL BE ROUND TO MARK THEM.

SSH!

She's the very PEST for laughs! She's . . .

Seems that everyone cowers—when the Peril picks flowers!

Stand by! Some more scrappin'—is all set to happen!

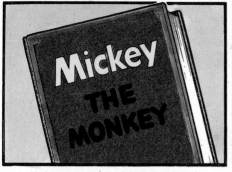

NICK KELLY

AND HIS ASSISTANT **Cedric**

IN THE CASE OF THE **SLICK OIL THIEVES**

WE'LL FILL UP WITH PETROL AT THIS GARAGE, MR KELLY. IT'S THE CHEAPEST PLACE IN TOWN.

I DON'T KNOW HOW THEY DO IT—IT'S ONLY HALF PRICE!

GARAGE PE

50% OFF

JUST THEN, BY CAR-RADIO—

CALLING NICK KELLY. REPORT TO THE MINISTER OF SECRET INFORMATION RIGHT AWAY.

LET'S MOVE, CEDRIC—SOUNDS LIKE AN URGENT CASE FOR US.

THE MINISTER IS EXPECTING YOU, MR KELLY.

PRIVATE

MINISTRY OF SECRET INFORMATION

WALLS HAVE EARS

. . . SEEMS THAT SOMETHING'S WRONG AT ONE OF OUR NORTH SEA OIL WELLS. THE RIG KEEPS PUMPING THE OIL UP—BUT NONE OF IT IS COMING ASHORE.

A LEAK, MINISTER?

NO, WE'VE CHECKED. IT'S A MOST BAFFLING AFFAIR, KELLY. GO TO IT.

SO, SOON—

LET'S HEAD FOR THAT RIG, THEN, CEDRIC.

I'VE GOT THE DIVERS' SUITS.

THAT'S THE RIG, SO THE OIL PIPE-LINE SHOULD BE ABOUT HERE.

SHONA PETERHEAD

THE PIPE LOOKS ALL RIGHT, SO FAR.

THEN—

LOOK! AN OLD SEA-CHEST.

DAVY JONES'S LOCKER? I DON'T BELIEVE IT.

DAVY JONES

WELL, I'M BLOWED! IT'S A CUNNING DISGUISE FOR A TAP INTO THE PIPE-LINE.

DAVY JONES

JUST THEN—

HELLO! A SUB! QUICKLY—HIDE, CEDRIC.

THEY'VE CONNECTED A PIPE TO THE TAP.

NOW I UNDERSTAND! THE OIL IS BEING PINCHED BY SUBMARINE PIRATES. HOW COULD THEY SINK SO LOW?

LET'S SLIP IN THROUGH THIS AIR-LOCK BEFORE THEIR DIVER RETURNS.

HATCH CLOSED, MR KELLY.

RIGHT! I'LL OPEN THE AIR LOCK.

NOW TO PLANT MY SPECIAL 'STENCHO' HOMING DEVICE SOMEWHERE, THEN WE'LL SLIP AWAY.

THERE! IT'S MAGNETIC, SO IT'LL STICK TO THIS STEEL PARTITION.

SUDDENLY—

AVAST, YE SWABS!

WE'RE SCUPPERED. RUN!

BACK THIS WAY.

GULP! WE'VE BLUNDERED INTO THE CREW'S QUARTERS.

STOWAWAYS! GRAB 'EM!

I'LL HAVE NO STOWAWAYS ABOARD MY SHIP! LET THEM TRAVEL BY TUBE— TORPEDO TUBE!

WE'RE GOING TO BE FIRED, CEDRIC.

FIRE ONE! FIRE TWO!

OOOW!

WHOOSH!

WHAT A STROKE OF LUCK! THERE'S OUR BOAT.

THOSE NASTY SUBMARINERS DIDN'T KNOW ABOUT THAT.

SOON—

ALMOST ASHORE. WE'LL NEED THE HELP OF THE COASTGUARDS TO TACKLE THIS CASE.

SHONA PETERHEAD

SHORTLY—

WE'LL DO ALL WE CAN TO HELP, MR KELLY, BUT HOW WILL WE KNOW WHERE THOSE OIL PIRATES WILL SURFACE?

EASY, INSPECTOR. WE'LL SNIFF 'EM OUT, YOU'LL SEE.

H M COASTGUARD H M

MEANWHILE, ON THE PIRATE SUB—

STEER FOR OUR SECRET REFINERY. HO! HO! THAT'S ANOTHER LOAD OF CHEAP PETROL FOR US TO SELL OFF.

SUDDENLY, KELLY'S 'STENCHO' HOMING DEVICE GOES OFF—

HISSSS!

COO! WHAT A PONG!

PHEWEE! IT'S 'ORRIBLE!

THE STORY OF WILLIAM ROBIN TELL HOOD
(OR SOMEBODY VERY LIKE HIM)

PHEW! IT'S HARD WORK TRANSPLANTING THESE APPLE TREES!

WILLIAM BECAME FAMOUS WHEN HE SHOT AN APPLE TREE OFF HIS FATHER'S HEAD—

WHO DID THAT?

CLOP!

WILLIAM TELL NO LIES—IT WAS I!

I'M GLAD YOU'RE HONEST, BUT I'M STILL GONNA THUMP YOU FOR THAT CORNY JOKE.

SO WILLIAM RAN AWAY . . .

. . . AND LIVED IN A FOREST WITH HIS FRIENDS, ABRAHAM LINCOLN GREEN AND LITTLE JOHN SILVER.

THEY ROBBED THE RICH AND GAVE TO THE POOR—

CHEER UP! YOUR TURN IN THE POOR QUEUE TOMORROW!

RICH QUEUE

POOR QUEUE

WILLIAM KEPT FIT BY JOGGING THROUGH THE FOREST, THUS HE CAME TO BE KNOWN AS PUFFING BILLY, WHICH GAVE HIM AN IDEA . . .

PUFF! PUFF! PUFF! PUFF!

THERE! THE WORLD'S FIRST STEAM-ENGINE!

HISS!

. . . THIS MADE HIM VERY RICH . . .

'BOUT TIME YOU INVENTED THAT— WE'VE BEEN WAITING FIVE YEARS!

HISS!

HISS!

. . . SO HE BOUGHT HIS FATHER A BIG, NEW APPLE TREE, AND THEY BOTH LIVED IN IT TO A RIPE OLD AGE!

THE TEENY TOPPERS

SUE

LOU

HUGH

IT'S A LOVELY DAY FOR A PICNIC AT CRUMBLY CASTLE.

OH, IT LOOKS LIKE RAIN! WHAT A PITY! HAR! HAR!

GLOORSH!

↑ BERTRAM BOVVER, THE BULLY NEXT DOOR.

SPLOOSH!

WHAT ARE THEY UP TO, NOW?

TO WORK, TEAM!

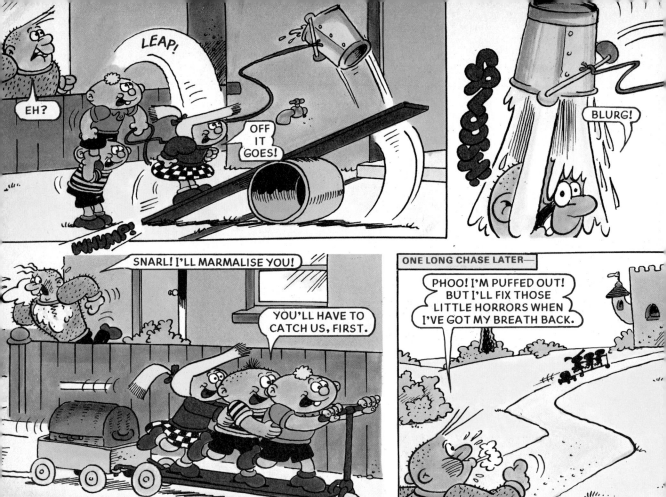

WE'LL FIX YOUR LIGHTS AND STUFF WHEN WE RETURN. BUT WE'VE COME TO TAKE YOU ON A QUICK TRIP YOU CAN'T MISS.

WHAT'S IT ALL ABOUT?

THE ZERAPIAN GROK!

THE WHAT?

By now, the boys were aboard the Whizzers' amazing little Whizz-car, shooting through space almost as fast as the speed of light!

GROKS ARE ALMOST EXTINCT. THIS ONE LIVES ALONE ON A PLANETOID WHICH ORBITS THROUGH OZZ SPACE ONLY ONCE IN TEN THOUSAND YEARS.

WE'LL NEVER HAVE ANOTHER CHANCE TO SEE IT.

But, when they reached the Ozz nebula—

OH, NO! THAT'S A KETT AUTOMATIC HANGAR IN ORBIT!

THE KETTS MUST BE AFTER THE GROK!

The Ketts were members of a criminal race who also lived on planet Ozz.

Krik swiftly landed the Whizz-car on the planetoid.

GROKS' SKINS ARE THE MOST VALUABLE TREASURE IN THE KETTS' HOME LAND.

GOSH! WE CAN'T LET THEM CAPTURE IT! WE'D BETTER FIND IT FIRST!

HOORAY! THERE'S THE GROK!

COMMANDER, WE HAVE SPOTTED THE BEAST.

Willie and the Whizzer twins hadn't yet seen several small ships coming from the opposite direction!

There was just one problem—

NOW WE'VE TO GET THE GROK TO THE OZZPROTECTOR ZONE, WHERE HE CAN LIVE IN PEACE.

HOW CAN WE DO THAT?

WITH WHIZZ-FOIL!

WE'LL WRAP THE GROK IN IT, FOR HIS JOURNEY THOUGH SPACE!

Soon, the Grok was securely wrapped up in the make-shift space-suit.

HERE, BOY—HAVE AN ENERGY WHIZZ-CHOC!

NEXT, WE NEED A GROK-SIZED SPACE HELMET!

A nozzle slid from a side panel on the Whizz-car, and a bubble began to appear.

Very soon, it was "Grok-sized"!

THESE GAS GLOBES WILL LIFT HIM FREE OF THE ASTEROID'S GRAVITY.

A PERFECT FIT!

YOU CAN RIDE ON THE GROK'S BACK, WILLIE.

SUPER!

His pipes bring things to life! Meet . . .

Peter Piper

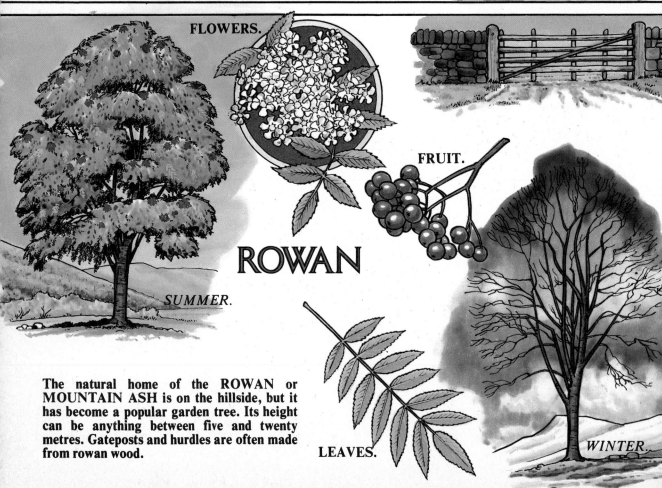

LEAVES.

NUTS.

WALNUT

WINTER.

BUDS and CONES.

SUMMER.

The **WALNUT** is a very sturdy tree and sometimes reaches a height of over thirty metres. In Europe, it is mainly grown for its fruit, but the fine-grained timber is also used for making gun-stocks and furniture.

FLOWERS.

FRUIT.

ROWAN

SUMMER.

LEAVES.

WINTER.

The natural home of the **ROWAN** or **MOUNTAIN ASH** is on the hillside, but it has become a popular garden tree. Its height can be anything between five and twenty metres. Gateposts and hurdles are often made from rowan wood.

LEAVES and FRUIT. (Acorns.)

OAK

WINTER.

SUMMER.

FLOWERS.

The mighty OAK is the biggest and best-known of Britain's trees. A full-grown oak may be over forty metres high. Oak timber has great strength and is particularly valuable in boat-building.

BUDS.

LIME

LEAVES and FLOWERS.

FRUIT.

SUMMER.

WINTER

The LIME grows well in parkland and meadows. It is a popular tree for city streets and avenues. The lime tree grows to a height of over twenty-five metres, and the wood is very suitable for carving.

SOUPER BOY

AUNT MAISIE'S COMING TO VISIT US! HERE'S HER TRAIN NOW!

HI, AUNTIE . . . YIKES! IT DIDN'T STOP!

HOOT!

THUNDER!

SWOOSH!

SCREECH! HELP!

I GET THE FEELING SOMETHING'S WRONG!

POW!

ED'S NOTE:— YOU DON'T SAY!

VOOM!

ZAP!

TIME FOR SOUPER BOY TO INVESTIGATE.

FIRST THING TO DO IS CHECK WITH THE DRIVER!

SOUPER-ZOOM!

DO SOMETHING, SOUPER BOY! THE BRAKES HAVE FAILED!

TUSH! TUSH!

R.B.

The chap below—has nowhere to go!

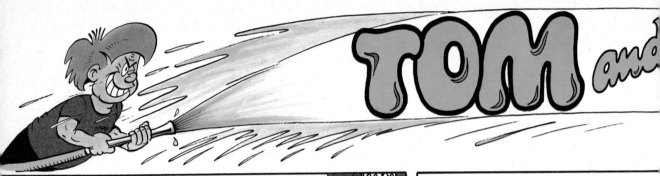

TOM and

HERE YOU ARE, TOM. YOU CAN CLEAN THE CAR.

EH? HUH! I THOUGHT WE WERE SUPPOSED TO BE ON HOLIDAY!

BAH! IT'S ALL RIGHT FOR TERRY! SHE CAN DO WHAT SHE LIKES 'COS SHE'S A GIRL!

YOU ROTTER! WHAT WAS **THAT** FOR?

I'M FED-UP! DAD'S MAKING ME WASH THE CAR.

WHY DIDN'T YOU SAY? I'LL HELP— FOR HALF OF WHAT DAD PAYS YOU.

OKAY. I'LL FIX UP THE HOSE.

C'MERE AND GET PUNCHED!

TEE-HEE! HAW! HAW! HAW!

TOSS!

FINISHED THE CAR, THEN, TOM?

YES, DAD! I DID IT— ER—ALL BY MYSELF.

OOF!

SHOVE!

TERRY

...END!

H'MM... HER NECK COULD DO WITH A WASH.

BULLSEYE!

YEEK!

SLORP!

...ACKLE! I CAN'T RESIST THIS!

DEEDLE-DEE-DEE-DUM-DAH!

WOO-HOORF! GOTCHA!

OOSHKLE! I'LL GET YOU FOR THAT!

SLOOSH!

AARGH!

GURGLE! THE WATER WAS STILL ON WHEN I CHUCKED THE HOSE AWAY!

SLOORSH!

LATER—

THAT'LL TEACH THE PEST! IF YOU FINISH CLEANING THE CAR, TERRY, I'LL PAY YOU INSTEAD.

HO! HO! TOM'S LOOKING SLIGHTLY WASHED-OUT!

Sir Vernon The Valiant

THE SHORTEST KNIGHT IN THE KINGDOM.

Seems EVERYONE loses—with each hobby she chooses!

BERYL the PERIL

ARE COLD AFTER BEING ON TRAFFIC DUTY!
STOMP!
CLOMP!
WHAT'S AFOOT?
THE MIGHTY FEET OF P.C. STAMPER
DOWN BELOW—
OORF! P.C. STAMPER IS SHAKING BITS OFF THE ROOF.
IT'S STOPPED. LOOKS LIKE HE'S MOVED ON.
BUT—
NOPE! HE'S STILL THERE. WE'LL HAVE TO TAKE ACTION!
PHEEEEP!
FROM ALL ROUND, INSECTS ANSWER THE CALL—
CHARGE, CHEPS!
JAB!
CLOMP!
THUMP!
THONK!
BOP! BOP! BOP!
BOP! BOP!
CLUNK!
THUNK!
THIS'LL GET RID OF HIM!
OOH! I'VE GOT PINS AN' NEEDLES IN ME FEET—THAT ALWAYS HAPPENS WHEN THE FEELING'S COMING BACK!

NICK KELLY

AND HIS ASSISTANT

CEDRIC

IN THE CASE OF THE

HI-JACKED HORSE

GO ON, BROWN BOMBER! YOU'RE WINNING.

SUDDENLY—

GOOD GRIEF! SOMEONE'S BACKED A HORSE-BOX ON TO THE COURSE, MR KELLY.

BROWN BOMBER'S CHARGING STRAIGHT INTO IT, CEDRIC.

AND—

EEK!

RIGHT, PATRICK! DRIVE ON!

THEY'VE KIDNAPPED BROWN BOMBER JUST AS HE WAS ABOUT TO WIN THE RACE.

AND WE HAD A WINNING TICKET!

QUICK—LET'S BORROW THIS ANIMAL AND FOLLOW THOSE HORSE-SNATCHERS.

YOU DRIVE, MR KELLY.

HEY!

HORSE-THIEVES! WHAT BOUNDERS!

THE HORSE-BOX TRACKS LEAD TOWARDS THAT FARM.

WE'VE DONE ALL WE CAN TODAY, SO LET'S BOOK IN HERE FOR THE NIGHT.

YE OLDE INNE

BED-TIME

THUMP! THUD!

BAH! WE'VE GOT NOISY GUESTS IN THE ROOM ABOVE, MR KELLY.

I'LL SAY!

SUDDENLY

A HORSE'S LEG?

OUCH!

UP ABOVE

STUPID HORSE! YOU'VE GIVEN THE GAME AWAY! I'LL LOCK THE DOOR THEN TRY TO HIDE YOU SOMEWHERE.

← BROWN BOMBER

BUT WHEN KELLY AND CEDRIC BURST IN . . .

WHUMP!

OUCH!

CHARGE!

YOU WERE RIGHT, CEDRIC. IT WAS A HORSE'S LEG, AND THERE HE IS, TUCKED UP IN BED!

AND THERE'S THE NASTY HORSE-SNATCHER!

PRESENTLY

A CUSTOMER FOR YOU, SERGEANT.

POLICE

WELL DONE, KELLY! ANOTHER CASE SOLVED, EH?

LATER, AT ANOTHER RACE MEETING . . .

YIPPEE! BROWN BOMBER'S WON.

HE'S A WONDER HORSE.

FANTASTIC FUN - TALES
IT'S TIME YOU WERE TOLD THE TRUTH ABOUT OLDE FATHER TIME

YEP—OLD FATHER TIME, THAT'S ME, FOLKS!

THAT'S HOW MOST PEOPLE THINK OF OLD FATHER TIME. BUT TIME—AHEM!—IS PASSING FOR HIM, TOO!

THIS STUFF'S WORN OUT!

...AND 1829 TO 1984!

I SAY—WHO'S PINCHED MY RAILWAY TRACKS?

RUMBLE!

S- STEVENSON'S ROCKET?

AT THE SAME TIME—

HOWDY, PARD! FUNNY-LOOKIN' HORSE YOU GOT THERE!

YERP!

1815—

BY ZE PLUME OF MY TENT! ZIS IS NOT MY WATERLOO!

STICK 'EM UP!

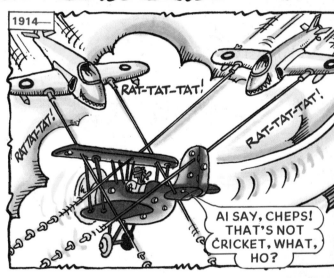

1914—

RAT-TAT-TAT!

RAT-TAT-TAT!

RAT-TAT-TAT!

AI SAY, CHEPS! THAT'S NOT CRICKET, WHAT, HO?

I'LL TAKE THIS.

THAT BE FORTY GROATS, IF YE PLEASE!

NAILS

AND—

JEWELLERS

I'LL TAKE YOUR SHOP DISPLAY SIGN, IF YOU DON'T MIND.

CERTAINLY, SIR.

FLOWERS.

LARCH

LEAVES
and
CONES.

WINTER.

The LARCH grows best on mountain slopes. It is usually at least twenty-five metres high, and is one of Britain's most valuable trees. Among other things, the wood is used for telegraph poles and boat-building. Turpentine also comes from the larch. Unlike other conifers, it is not an evergreen.

BUDS
and
FLOWERS.

ASH

FRUIT.

SUMMER.

WINTER.

LEAVES.

The ASH is most plentiful on moist, low-lying land, where it often grows to well over thirty metres. Ash timber is very strong and flexible, and is used in the making of gliders, tool shafts and hockey sticks.

HORSE CHESTNUT

FLOWERS.

WINTER.

NUT.

FRUIT.
(Conkers.)

SUMMER.

The **HORSE-CHESTNUT** is found mainly in parks and gardens. Its growth is very rapid, and a full-grown tree may be thirty metres high. Its timber is even-grained and is used in toy and cabinet making.

ELM

FLOWERS
and
BUDS.

SUMMER

FRUIT.

LEAVES.

WINTER.

The **COMMON ELM** is found in all parts of the British Isles, but most frequently in lowlands and valleys, where it sometimes attains a height of forty metres. Its wood does not splinter easily, and was once widely used for making wheelbarrows and farm implements.

DANNY'S TRANNY

HI, FOLKS! TIME FOR ANOTHER TRANNY TALE.

IT WAS A GREAT IDEA TO FIT SKIS TO OUR BIKES, DANNY.

HEH- HEH! YEAH! HOW TO GO CYCLING IN THE SNOW, IN ONE EASY LESSON!

BUT, AHEAD, IN AMBUSH—

I'LL GIVE THAT DANNY WILSON A SHOCK!

ZONK!

OOH!

HAR! HAR!

A SPOT OF GROWING RAY ON THE BIKE WILL FIX THAT THIEVIN' BULLY!

GROWING RAY LW

QUICKLY THEN, DANNY.

THANKS, CHUM. I'LL BE 'SKIING' YOU! HO! HO!

SUDDENLY—

ZONK!

UGH!

HELP!

GOT MY BIKE BACK. NOW, LET'S GO!

PRESENTLY—

LOOK! THAT CAR'S SKIDDING! IT'S GOING TO CRASH INTO THAT LORRY.

ANOTHER QUICK JOB FOR THE TRANNY!

SKID!

YOU'VE SHRUNK IT!

SHRINKING RAY V SW!

AB1280

PHEW! THE TINY CAR CAN SCOOT SAFELY NOW UNDER THE LORRY.

BUT—

HELP!

OH, DEAR! IT'S ENDED UPSIDE-DOWN IN THE DITCH!

BACK TO NORMAL

GOTTA RESCUE THE POOR DRIVER—AND FAST!

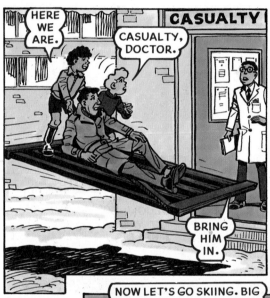

Desert Island Dick

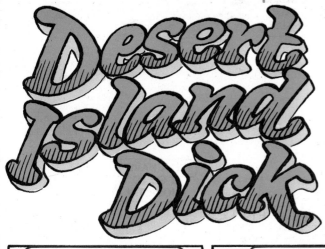

TRICKY DICKY

ROVER, HERE, IS A VERY SPECIAL BREED OF DOG! HE'S GOT A BIT OF EVERYTHING IN HIM. CACKLE!

HOO! HOO! WHAT A FUNNY-LOOKING DOG! DOES HE BITE?

NOPE!

HE PUNCHES! Y'SEE, HE'S A BOXER! HAR! HAR!

BLAARGHLE!

SOCK!

PRESS!

HELLO, NICE DOGGUMS! I THINK YOU'RE A SPANIEL!

TWEET!

PAT!

HORACE

LEAVES.

SILVER BIRCH

FEMALE CATKINS.

MALE CATKINS.

SUMMER.

WINTER.

The SILVER BIRCH will grow in almost any kind of soil, and it is a common tree throughout Britain. It is rarely more than twenty-five metres high. Birch timber is very hard and was once especially popular for making railway wagons.

SCOTS PINE

LEAVES and CONES.

SILVER FIR

CONE.

LEAVES.

The SCOTS PINE and the SILVER FIR are both evergreens, which may grow to more than thirty metres high. The bark of the Scots pine is rough and reddish-coloured, while that of the Silver fir is smooth and grey. Timber from these trees is used for rafters, flooring, and other interior woodwork.

LEAVES.

FLOWERS.
(May Blossom).

SUMMER.

HAWTHORN

WINTER

BUDS
and
THORNS.

The tangled, thorny branches of the HAWTHORN make it an ideal hedge tree. In this form it rarely grows to any great height, but individual trees, growing on open ground, have been known to reach a height of fifteen metres. Hawthorn wood is very tough, and is used for stakes.

FLOWERS.

COPPER BEECH

LEAVES.

WINTER.

FRUIT.

SUMMER.

The COPPER BEECH is easily recognised by its copper or purple-coloured leaves. It is a tall tree, frequently more than twenty-five metres high. The wood of this tree is hard and heavy, and is ideal for tools.

Candy floss makes Ali cross!

HERE ARE SOME CHARACTERS YOU *DIDN'T* MEET IN THIS BOOK!